Antique Chinese Rugs

RUG OF "THE HUNDRED ANTIQUES"

The field of this rug is of a rich deep apricot color and the designs upon it are woven in light and dark blue, two shades of yellow and a reddish brown. A limiting border of corrosive dye surrounds the entire rug. The objects which fill the field are copies of old bronzes, porcelains, and various other articles precious to the Chinese. Many of these are outlined in contrasting colors and bear decorations of significance. There are scrolls, books, altar implements, tripods, vases of flowers, brush holders, ink-stones, a chessboard, branches of coral, a lute, incense, vases, basins and stands carrying plants and fungus growths, a rhinoceros horn, jade charms, etc. In the main border a dark blue swastika fret is laid upon a ground color of apricot which has faded to a soft dull yellow. Imposed upon this fret are flower forms carrying signs of "shou." Bands of yellow and two shades of blue separate the main border from the field.

[No. 5600—10.3 × 5.8]

Antique Chinese Rugs

by the Tiffany Studios

CHARLES E. TUTTLE COMPANY: PUBLISHERS
Rutland, Vermont & Tokyo, Japan

Representatives
Continental Europe: BOXERBOOKS, INC., *Zurich*
British Isles: PRENTICE-HALL INTERNATIONAL, INC., *London*
Australasia: PAUL FLESCH & CO., PTY. LTD., *Melbourne*
Canada: M. G. HURTIG LTD., *Edmonton*

Published by the Charles E. Tuttle Company, Inc.
of Rutland, Vermont & Tokyo, Japan
with editorial offices at Suido 1-chome, 2–6
Bunkyo-ku, Tokyo, Japan

Copyright in Japan 1969 by Charles E. Tuttle Co., Inc.

Library of Congress Catalog Card No. 69-16178

Standard Book No. 8048 0025-1

First Tuttle edition published 1969

PRINTED IN JAPAN

CONTENTS

LIST OF PLATES

LIST OF PLATES

PUBLISHER'S FOREWORD

AN attractive volume containing 33 plates, this is a reprint of the third book in a series put out by the Tiffany Studios of New York City in 1908.

It is a "selection of beautiful and interesting specimens, which in color, design and age form a collection pre-eminent in this country and probably not equaled in the world."

The classification of rugs depends upon the recognition of certain technical peculiarities that they possess. These peculiarities make it possible to place the rugs in a certain period of time with considerable accuracy.

Chinese rugs are recognizable by characteristic designs, chief of these being mythological, naturalistic and geometric, and they have been copied through the centuries. Some of the rugs have archaic dragons in the corners and borders. Others show books, lutes, chessboards, scrolls, and the significant peach, pomegranate, and other fruit.

More than a collection of illustrations and accompanying text, this enticing work also describes the historic periods in Chinese art, the materials used in the rugs and the methods of weaving;

colors and design; classification according to color and design, and an expert and complete description of the plates.

Each beautiful rug is a story in itself, has a nobility of its own, worth tracing and studying like a magnificent colored map. The clue to certain designs at certain periods must be found in the history of the empire itself. As an example, Mohammedan designs are found in the products of the Kien-lung period. The reason: one of the favorites of Kien-lung was a Kashgarian princess.

This book offers infinite possibilities for scholarly enjoyment as well as aesthetic pleasures for the true art lover.

PREFACE

THE classifications of Chinese rugs adopted by different students must necessarily vary. As there are no existing records of the evolution of the Chinese weaver's art, its traditional history can play no part in the formation of opinions. Therefore the classification of rugs must depend upon the recognition of certain technical peculiarities in them. These peculiarities reveal methods that either antedate or follow other methods of which we have a knowledge which makes it possible to place objects relatively with a great amount of accuracy. The technical peculiarities that support trained opinion have been explained in the following chapters. They have to do with materials used by weavers, with the colors of these materials, and with the various methods of weaving them.

IT may readily be seen, as has been demonstrated, that designs in rugs admit of entirely different classification from that of the fabrics themselves. Only when both weaving and design are studied together is substantial evidence acquired that will corroborate all theories in regard to the time and place of manufacture, for the same designs were used by weavers who lived centuries apart. The effect of time and age on materials and colors must be noted before classing any fabric as antique, however old the design may be. In adopting five periods as indicative of five great styles in Chinese weavings, the Tiffany Studios have so grouped the rugs in their collection that they may illustrate the theories advanced, which are based upon careful analysis and comparison. The spelling of Chinese words adopted by the Tiffany Studios in the naming and classification of rugs is as far as possible that used by distinguished scholars who have written in English of things Chinese. When such authorities differ, choice has been made of words as they have been most commonly employed by collectors.

Starred numbers in the text refer to rugs illustrated in the plates; unstarred numbers, to other rugs in the Tiffany Studios Collection.

M. C. R.

CHAPTER I.

HISTORIC PERIODS IN
CHINESE ART.

AT whatever actual time the Chinese
rugs were made which now exist in
collections and museums, the designs
used by their makers may be readily classed
as belonging to one or another of five great
styles that have made Chinese art what it is.

LOOKING into the remote past for the
influences that produced the first of
the great styles, we find convincing
evidence that, on ancient bronzes and
sacrificial vessels and implements used by
Confucianists and Taoists, the designs mythological, naturalistic and geometric are to be
found, which have been copied all through
the centuries. These designs were native to

China, had to do with ancestor worship and the worship of heaven and earth, and were elemental and crude in conception and execution; but as they were originally drawn they were often copied in facsimiles of later date.

WITH the entrance of Buddhism into China during the first century of our era, the great flood of new thought brought about changes in existing ornament, and developed much that was entirely new, making the second period in the styles in Chinese ornament. With Buddhism came the decorative impulse, and though the new cult seized much that it found ready for its adoption, it also added new ideas that were easily grafted upon the native stock; and whether or not some of the features ordinarily claimed to be Buddhist antedated the Christian era, it is true that the designs created by Buddhism are different from those of the earlier period.

DURING the Sung dynasty, the third of the great styles developed. The philosophers of the eleventh and twelfth centuries reverted to the past in their

PLATE I.

a. Archaic Bronze Sacrificial Urn.

b. Border from Chinese rug, with archaic
dragon, geometric and foliate
ornamentation.

studies, and their comments and conclusions furnished art with a net-work of ideas, from which many intricate philosophical and occult designs evolved. Neither the entrance of Mohammedan, Roman Catholic or Mongolian ideas materially changed the historic ornament of China prior to the Sung dynasty. The motifs they supplied were mingled with those of later periods into which they merged.

THE Ming dynasty gave birth to the fourth period in the styles of Chinese ornament, and during its continuance, from the middle of the fourteenth to the middle of the seventeenth century, both Mohammedan and European influences marked art in many ways. During this period there was employed in art work a superlative abundance of decorative schemes. Objects of rare beauty were made at the instigation of the Ming emperors, and art reached its high water mark in China.

THE fifth great epoch in the production of Chinese styles began with the Emperor K'ang-hsi of the present Tartar dynasty, and extended for one hundred years until the latter part of the eighteenth century. The influence of Persia and the middle Orient was felt very much during this period, and differentiated its ornament from all that had gone before.

THE historic ornament of China as applied to the decoration of rugs may be divided into these five great styles. From these styles weavers have appropriated the designs best adapted to the limitations of their looms, and oftentimes, when ornament as applied to some other of the industrial arts is copied by weavers, great freedom is noticeable in the handling of designs. The arts are interdependent, and the objects produced by jade, ivory, and wood carvers, bronze mirror makers and potters have furnished rug weavers with many of their most attractive inspirations. These five styles may be subdivided, contracted or extended for specific purposes, but the broad classification is all that is necessary in the study of rugs.

PLATE II.

a. Dragon-fret square.

[5115—2.9×2.10]

b. Geometric-fret square.

[5462—2.9×2.5]

CHAPTER II.

MATERIALS USED IN
CHINESE RUGS.

THE Chinese rugs which are available
for examination and study to-day,
about which expert students have a
right to speculate, and in regard to which
trained opinion is of great value, are made
with a pile of either fine or coarse wool,
hair, or silk, seldom if ever of either cotton
or jute. Sometimes the wool is so coarse
that it has the appearance of jute, and rugs
are often classified as jute that are in reality
of coarse hair or wool. Japanese rugs that
imitate Persian and Chinese are made of
cotton or jute, and need not be mistaken for
the products which they imitate, as they are

distinctive and may be very easily placed.

ALTHOUGH it is generally possible to determine at a glance the material used in the pile of Chinese rugs, it is necessary to remove a single knot from the rug and untwist it in order to come to definite conclusion in regard to the methods employed in the preparation of the materials. Hand spinning is easily detected, as it is generally possible to pull apart the filaments and turn the wool back again into its original condition when it has been crudely prepared by domestic process, whereas it is quite impossible to do this with machine twisted wool, hair, or silk, which has been stretched and drawn out of all resemblance to natural wool or cocoon silk. The test of burning is absolute and one has only to burn cotton, silk, wool and hair, one after the other, in order to be able to see the variations in the way fire affects the different products. The sense of smell aids that of sight, burning wool emitting a vastly different odor from either cotton or silk. With these methods at hand for drawing definite conclusions, it is comparatively easy to avoid all mistakes in the classification of materials.

PLATE III.

Archaic dragon rug.

[5132—5.11 × 3.11]

THE nature of the hair in Chinese rugs varies. Camel's hair is easily recognized, both in superior and inferior grades. There is a softness and spring to the hairs, and, under a strong glass, variations in their size are noticeable. Many Chinese rugs are made of a coarse hair which resembles cow's hair. These are generally known as Yak rugs in the Occident and are readily distinguishable, whatever animal actually yielded the hair used in their manufacture. The use to-day of certain materials leads to the inference that the same were used in the past. This conclusion is useful as it enables one to classify the rugs to-day in collections either public or private.

THE pile in many of the most interesting rugs that have been made in China is of very coarse hair twisted with the most ordinary grade of wool. These rugs generally bear designs which correspond in crudity with the material used in their manufacture. The wools in Chinese rugs vary and admit of careful analysis. In rugs made prior to the nineteenth century the wools seem to have greater spring, vigor and glint than those which were made during the last century by more refined processes.

WHEN very soft wool loosely twisted is used in early Ming fabrics, several strands are found in each knot tied, which as they untwist make a fine surface almost like velvet. While wool is used in the weft and sometimes in the warp in rugs of the Western part of the Chinese Empire and in Tibet, we rarely if ever find a wool web in the rugs of Eastern China. Cotton very crudely prepared appears in warp and woof in Chinese rugs both coarse and fine but cotton is very rarely used in the pile. This material has been adopted by the Japanese, who closely imitate in cotton and jute the wool and silk rugs of China, Persia and other parts of the Orient.

TECHNICAL methods of preparing materials become apparent to the trained eye. The careful cleansing of natural products, while it refines them, sometimes takes from the charm of crude methods of preparation. Loose spinning and irregular yarn indicate that the fabric was made before

the introduction of process work of any kind
in the place of its manufacture, and though
labor is simplified and reduced by mechanical
means, there is a vastly different appearance
to rugs made under modern factory control
from those produced independently by
domestic process. The same conclusions may
be drawn regarding the preparation of silk.
Hard and compact surfaces are produced by
the use of carefully prepared silk while soft
and crude effects are due to the use of inferior grades of silk and often to the use of a raw
tram silk spun direct from the cocoons. This
analysis, while in no way adding to or taking
from the appreciation of the beauty of a
rug, aids materially in determining its age.

PLATE IV.

Mirror back rug.
[5454—6.5 × 4.3]

CHAPTER III.

METHODS OF WEAVING
CHINESE RUGS.

THE Chinese observe the ordinary methods employed all through the Orient in the weaving of pile carpets, the difference in the finished product being due to slight technical variations that serve as ear-marks for identification. These may be noted in the warp and woof threads, and in the way the knots, the ends of which make the pile, are tied. Even without actual historical records of how and when Chinese fabrics were made, it is quite possible to divide existing specimens in such a way as to determine the relation of one fabric to another; the changes from domestic to factory weaving and preparation of materials being quite apparent to the analyst.

IN many old rugs the warp threads are of soft loosely twisted cotton, the threads varying in thickness, and there are only about six or eight warp threads to an inch, even in rugs that appear on the surface to be fine and compactly woven. The woof threads in such rugs generally separate only three rows of knots to the inch and are held in place by warp threads which have been separated for their insertion by most primitive methods. It is quite possible to note that in making the yarn used for these woof threads, the cotton has been twisted by twirling the shaft between the fingers and the thumb in a very primitive way. The shuttles that have been used to separate warp threads in antique rugs made for ordinary use were, judging from the work accomplished by them, clumsy and large and incapable of producing fine and compact work.

WITH the refinement of implements and processes a loss as well as a gain has been accomplished, virility and simplicity of conception giving place at times to less vigor with advance in skill. Sometimes several woof threads are twisted loosely

PLATE V.

Abacus rug.
[5581—6.6×3.9]

PLATE VI.

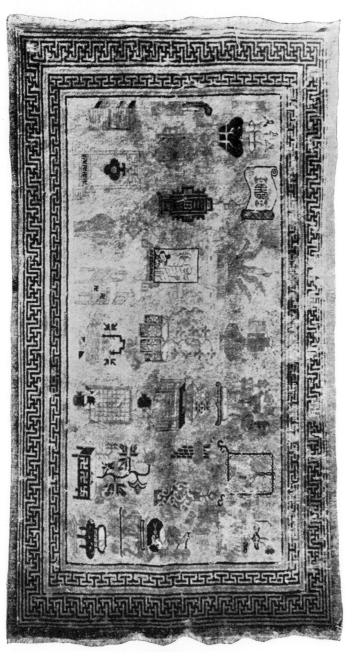

Po-Ku rug.
[5509—9.3 × 5.3]

together before they are wound on the shuttle, and after taking their places in the web they separate and appear like four threads, even when the shuttle is only thrown back and forth once between each two rows of knots. This description has to do with the rugs of Eastern China. The rugs of Western China and of Chinese Turkestan, and many of the rugs of Manchuria, of Northern China and the "cold countries" carry woof threads of wool and in some instances the entire web is woven of wool strands for both warp and woof.

THE knots in Chinese pile weaving are made by carrying the yarn under one strand (A) of the warp and over the second strand (B), which it surrounds, the end to appear between the two threads A and B. This gives a knot end between every two warp threads. In parting the pile on the surface, it is possible to expose one of every pair of warp threads (thread A for example) as only one strand of each pair is encircled completely by the pile wool. With Turkish knots it is impossible to do this, as both strands of each pair of the warp threads are

encircled. Chinese knots are tied exactly as Persian or Sinneh knots, differing from them in appearance simply because of the more slazy quality of the loose web.

IN silk rugs, warp, woof and pile are apt to be of silk, though sometimes, to cheapen the product, the woof strands are of cotton. The weft in some very old silk rugs consists of coarse silk, about which a strong silk thread is twisted. Some of the fine silk rugs of the Ming dynasty show this interesting feature.

THERE are certain technical peculiarities in weaving that have produced styles now known as Ming, K'ang-hsi, Yung-cheng, Kien-lung and Tao-kuang. In the classification of Chinese rugs, allusion is more often made to monarchs than to centuries, for styles evolved under the patronage of one or another sovereign, and these styles, with the influence upon them of foreign conquest and intercourse with other nations, eventually resulted in producing the various schemes adopted by weavers.

PLATE VII.

Geometric dragon medallion rug.
[5576—8.6 × 5.4]

ARLY Ming rugs divide themselves into two classes — those made at the behest of royalty for the private use of princes and sovereigns, and those that were made for ordinary domestic or temple use. There are fine old silk fabrics with a close-cut pile resembling velvet, which illustrate different methods of weaving — one method being that of making the rug entirely of silk, by tying the knots which make the pile upon a silk warp which is penetrated between each two rows of knots by a silk weft thread. Another, and the most commonly accepted method, was to make both warp and woof of cotton and only the pile of silk.

THE sumptuous rugs known as the metal and silk products of the Ming dynasty are among the most marvellous fruits of the loom. The design is shown in relief upon a flat background of metal, in which both gold and silver threads are used. This same general style of weaving obtains in other countries, but there are slight technical differences which reveal variations in the methods employed. In some rugs, for example, the metal forms the woof which penetrates the warp threads as in ordinary weaving and is packed so closely that it makes a solid appearance and a smooth metallic surface. In others, upon a web of cotton, a chain-stitch of metal thread is carried across from side to side of the rug, making an embroidered surface. The same appearance is obtained in the weavings of other parts of the Orient by encircling each warp thread by a single woof thread back and forth across the width of the stretched warp, producing a herringbone pattern.

THE name "Late Ming" is given to a style of rugs woven before Persian influence was strongly felt in the designs forced upon Chinese weavers. Only a few of the rugs thus classified are obtainable at the present time and in them the colors are soft and the general effect subdued. Yellow tan, which has faded from apricot, and two shades of blue, with a dark brown natural wool, are the only colors used in the pile of the late Ming rugs of this style.

BESIDE copying Ming styles, K'ang-shi rugs show Persian influence in design, and the color schemes, even where later designs are used, are similar to those of the late Ming period. Manchurian ideas and colors are noticeable in late K'ang-hsi rugs and in the Yung-cheng period such are included. With Kien-lung came the Turkestan, East Indian and Samarcand influences, as well as the development and demonstration of designs and methods purely Chinese, so that the Kien-lung period of sixty years, covering as it did the greater part of the eighteenth century, included in its products a reproduction of almost everything that had gone before, as well as much of additional interest and beauty.

EIGHTEENTH century weavings are distinguishable however from those of earlier periods, and the fabrics themselves must be relied upon to authenticate specimens. Broadly speaking then it is advisable to divide the antique rugs of China into five periods; first, sixteenth and seventeenth century Ming; second, K'ang-hsi; third, Yung-cheng; fourth, Kien-lung; fifth,

Tao-kuang or early nineteenth century. Rugs of the Kwang-su period, made during the last quarter of the nineteenth century, differ entirely from the factory and commercial rugs made to-day, and may be classed as native products and are often most beautiful and alluring.

PLATE VIII.

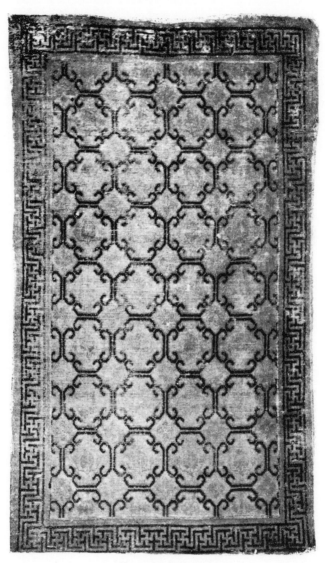

Longevity rug.
[5580—6.6×3.10]

CHAPTER IV

COLORS EMPLOYED BY CHINESE
WEAVERS.

CHINESE rugs *en masse* have a vastly
different appearance from a correspond-
ing number of Persian, Indian or
Turkish fabrics. Even when they are thrown
with rugs of other makes, it is possible to detect Chinese rugs at a glance.
Why this is so is perchance a debatable ques-
tion, though without doubt most students
who have given the subject any consideration
would not hesitate to say that it is due to the
lack in Chinese rugs of primary red, and the
substitution of varying secondary shades, such
as the fruit reds, apricot, persimmon, pomegranate and peach, that give the fabrics a
Chinese appearance in spite of the fact that

yellows and blues are often as strong and strictly primary in tone in Chinese as in other rugs.

THE colors employed by the Chinese differ from those used by Persian rug weavers, in that the Chinese palette is the smaller. Where the Persians would introduce a dozen tones, the Chinese content themselves with four or five. We find in rugs of one class two shades of yellow, two shades of blue and cream color. In another two shades of blue, cream color and apricot red. In another two shades of of yellow, two shades of cream and apricot. In another two shades of blue, cream, brown and two shades of yellow. A Persian rug classing with these would have yellow, two shades of blue, cream, several shades of green, fire-color, turquoise-blue and many shades of red. In Chinese rugs, however important, one fails to find many colors. The rugs of Chinese-Turkestan and of the Samarcand district lean toward Indian and Persian methods of introducing colors, but strictly Chinese rugs only show four or five tones.

IN studying the limited palette of the Chinese weaver it is interesting to begin with the use made of natural colored wools and hair. The fawn colors, which are strictly Chinese, differ somewhat from the tan colors of Hamadan camel's hair. The coarse hair of the yak, the cow and the other animals, and the wool both coarse and fine from native sheep, give endless variety to the quality of the materials used, which furnish the varying shades of fawn, tan, and light and dark brown in Chinese rugs.

A VERY dark brown that is sometimes found in Chinese rugs is of so corrosive a nature that the wool dyed with it is often entirely gone from rugs in which the wools of every other color are in perfect condition. We only occasionally find an old Chinese rug in which this peculiar shade of dark brown shows no wear whatever, and on examiuation the material proves to be of natural color and a blackish brown wool or hair. Such are without doubt the original color and material used, of which the brown, dyed with corrosive dye, is a copy. Colors found in existing antique specimens to-day are invaluable as guides to the study of the color scheme thought out by old weavers. Some of these shades accidentally obtained have never been equalled by the intentional mingling of colors, and have different values, according to the materials to which they are applied. There is however enough likeness between rugs of silk and those of wool of any period to make it possible to place them together, though the shades of color vary somewhat.

IN small fragments of very old Chinese rugs, and in copies of them, natural colored wools and hair are used in combination or in varying tones of the same color. Simple floral or symbolic objects are worked in a bleached white, while the body of the rug is of unbleached wool. Camel's hair is varied with dark wool and several shades of tan are so mingled as to show lines of solid colors surrounding a figured field.

BLUE in Chinese rugs when combined with white shows as varying results as does the mingling of the same colors in Chinese porcelains. To Chinese

PLATE IX.

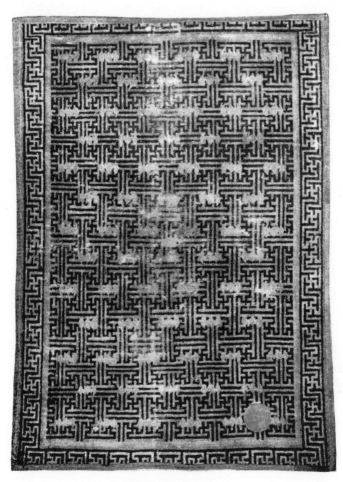

Happiness rug.
[5579—5.8 × 4.0]

blues many names have been applied which obtain with more or less accuracy. There is the indigo or deep strong blue found in the rugs of both Northern and Southern China, and the azure blue which is almost never found in rugs later than the eighteenth century. Sapphire blue found in Kien-lung Chinese-Turkestan rugs is unlike the light blue of either earlier or later periods. Silver blue appears in Peking rugs and grey blue in the products of Ning-hsi and the Northern provinces.

WITH white also we find limitless variations, so that a blue and white wool rug of China may show blue of any of the well known shades with quite as wide a range of tones in the white wool employed in the field. Cream and ash white, egg-shell white and clay color, grey white and putty color, silver white and *blanc de chine*, are a few of the numberless shades employed in making the so-called blue and white rugs of China and as in porcelains, so in textiles, never does the color known as the "blue shown in a rift in the clouds after rain" appear to such advantage as when blue is combined with the cloud white most closely related to it.

THE various shades of red are more difficult to define than any of the other colors employed by Chinese weavers. From whatever natural product they are obtained, they are of entirely different nature from the reds of any other country. Names that have been so often used as finally to seem of value and importance in classifying Chinese reds are pomegranate, persimmon, apricot, peach and fire color. The blood red found in old Samarcands and rugs of Turkestan and Tibet, never appears in the wool rugs of China, though occasionally a vivid ruby red is found in Chinese silk fabrics. Antique Chinese fruit reds are heavy with yellow and are utterly lacking in cerise and rose tints.

IMPERIAL yellow commands with Mandarin yellow the interest of all who endeavor to demonstrate the subtle differences that make for distinction and importance in the textiles of China. There is not an orange tint in the imperial yellow found in rugs, but there is enough red in the dye to prevent any verging toward lemon color, which of late years has distinguished modern products. Mandarin yellow favors orange color and yet differs entirely from fire-color in which there is almost as much orange color as red. No green is apparent in Chinese rugs that antedate the Kien-lung period, and only in rugs made after 1875 is there to be found the glaringly bad greenish yellow that at once testifies to the age of wools dyed with modern coal tar products. We look in vain for greens in Chinese rugs. When they appear at rare intervals they are of late date, and are seldom found in rugs woven east of Turkestan.

THE fugitive nature of some of the Chinese fruit reds causes them to fade out to a dull brown or yellow, and oftentimes a rug of tawny golden hue will upon close examination be found to have no yellow whatever in the pile, and the beautiful result has been brought about by the effect of time and slow fading, the yellow tones alone remaining after the vegetable or fruit reds have disappeared entirely. The dyers of

China at the present time mix with the twigs of logwood the juice of certain berries to give the yellow cast which characterizes Chinese reds. Any theories concerning ancient methods of dyeing materials in China are however largely speculative; and only with the present conditions of textiles is it possible to deal.

AS far as we are able to determine by study of the rugs of China themselves, there has been no servile allegiance whatever shown by weavers to the significance of colors. Chinese color symbolism is more accurate and direct than any of the ancient schemes for the use of colors, and in many branches of art it obtains and may be depended upon, though not in rug weaving. There are five colors considered sacred in China, each one supposed to be related to various natural objects and phenomena. One and another method is observed by authorities in the arrangement of these colors, the sequence most commonly accepted being black, green, red, white, yellow.

PLATE X.

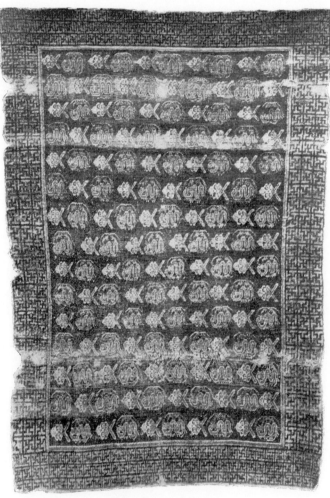

Magistrate's rug.

[4389—5.8 × 3.0]

CHAPTER V.

DESIGNS FOUND IN
CHINESE RUGS.

DESIGNS native and borrowed in Chinese rugs do not apparently belong to families, tribes or localities as they do in other parts of the Orient. The patriarchal nature of the native religions forced the use of certain objects in all parts of the Empire, which were made in stereotyped fashion and which bore accepted designs. It would appear that weavers copied the designs that had been thought out by craftsmen in the decoration of other objects long ago. These objects were presumably of bronze and to the sacrificial bronzes of early Chinese dynasties we may legitimately look for many of the designs which inspired both potters and weavers. However dissimilar may be the designs that cover the field in Chinese rugs, the border designs bear close resemblance to each other. In them, frets and formal arrangements of Chinese motifs antedate the foliate scroll ornament of the seventeenth and eighteenth centuries.

IN keeping to the five periods in the classification of Chinese rugs, it is possible to describe with a certain amount of accuracy the designs that are most often found in them. The field in many early Ming domestic products, in which the color tones are low and harmonious, carries an all-over design built upon the regular arrangement of well known and symbolic forms. The Joo-e often forms the design at the top, bottom and sides of spaces eight or ten inches square, the centers of which are filled with bats, peaches, or signs of longevity, happiness, or good luck. Octagon forms are sometimes spread over the entire field of a rug, carrying alternately coiled archaic dragon forms and some symbolic fruits. This repeat design is somewhat monotonous, at the same time in no other Chinese rugs are the results more harmonious and suggestive of native thought.

PLATE XI.

Metal and silk rug.
[4736—8.3 × 4.10]

PLATE XII.

Chinese Kirman rug.

[5599—5.0 × 2.9]

ANOTHER method of covering the field in early Ming rugs is to work the ground in solid color, upon which are distributed dots or stripes suggestive of tiger or leopard skins, which without doubt they copied. In the center of rugs of this class are large squares of another color, in which are grouped mythological objects most crudely drawn. Examination of the borders which commonly surround rugs of this special style is most helpful in determining the age of specimens, for when old styles are copied in the field, borders of late date are sometimes used. This often proves a rug to be a copy, which otherwise might have been considered an original.

IN early weavings the borders are few in number and not very wide — in fact in very early borders there appear only a few stripes, varying in color, around the entire fabric. In addition to these stripes, which were retained as outer or limiting band, an inner border was eventually added carrying a Swastika fret or some typically Chinese geometric form. Signs of "shou" and bats were used as over-laid ornaments upon these frets.   A favorite method of decoration with early weavers consisted in placing archaic dragon forms in conventional corner designs, and using the same motif in the central medallion, the borders in such rugs carrying elongated forms of the same dragon scroll.

IN the sumptuary metal and silk rugs of the Ming dynasty, weavers gave themselves greater license in every way.   Nothing more ornate, rich and extremely brilliant can be imagined than the rugs they produced.   To the art rather than the craft of the weaver do such belong, and in ordinary collections they are rarely seen. When they appear they explain themselves.

IN the K'ang-hsi period we find many different styles, each one more or less distinctive.   There is the carrying on of the tawny golden brown color scheme that obtains in the Ming styles, while the designs employed show distinctively Persian influence. The attempt at formalism which introduced radiating designs and a forcing of foreign motifs into compartments is an early K'ang-hsi method, but this was not fully developed

PLATE XIII.

Western Lotus rug.

[3459—5.10 × 3.8]

until later, when Kien-lung weavers adopted it and used it extensively. The Western Lotus appears in K'ang-hsi rugs, drawn in a way unlike any Chinese rendering of plant form prior to the latter part of the seventeenth century. This floral form with its accompanying stiffly-arranged foliation spreads over the field of rugs that carry border stripes of solid colors of about the same general tone as those employed in the field.

THE aster and peony are conventionalized for all-over decoration, in the same way that the lotus is used in this class of K'ang-hsi rugs, and are more suggestive of Persian influence than even the lotus design. More frequently too in the peony than in the lotus design, an attempt is made to introduce floral forms in the broad border stripe.

THE development of Yung-cheng and Manchurian styles shows, first, a mingling of earlier schemes with a freer use of both palette and decoration, succeeded later on by a definite style which bears the same relation to weaving as do the enamels of Peking to porcelains. Distinctly different was this method, which consisted in outlining the objects used in decoration with contrasting colors, the pile of the outline being clipped in such a way as to make a depression, which threw into relief the object it surrounded. Under whatever influence this style developed, it is known as Yung-cheng, and there are accounts in old records which testify to the fact that the copying of Peking enamels in the eighteenth century produced this result. The dark blue grounds, with floral decorations in cream, yellow and apricot, are presumably of the same period as those showing ribbed outlines and relief effects.

MANCHURIAN rugs made under royal patronage are closely woven, and in them are colors that differ from any found during the Ming period. In Manchurian rugs of the early eighteenth century, the designs assumed a regular style. Circular forms, or medallions, were placed at intervals over the field, which was covered with an indistinct swastika fret work. The use of geometric dragon forms in these medallions antedates the more frequently found conventionalized flowers. Dragon scrolls and frets were introduced in the border. In early Manchurian rugs, mythological and symbolic designs alternated with the floral arrangements that developed in the southern part of the Empire about the same time. Whether legitimately so or not, in the separation of Chinese rugs for purposes of trade classification, styles have been apportioned to different localities in China.

CANTON and Nankin products hold the same relation to each other in the output of textiles as of porcelains, in that a greater refinement is noticed in the designs of Nankin than in those of Canton. Cantonese trees, Cantonese rocks and teahouses, Cantonese renderings of Taoist ornament, Cantonese flowers differ from Nankin floral patterns, just as Canton Willow pattern porcelains differ from the same design painted in Nankin in the olden time, or as the Nankin design called " Fitzhugh " pattern differs from others more crudely drawn. In the weavings of the Shantung Province, designs adopted by weavers in all the other parts of the Empire have been copied, and in rugs bearing the name of Tien-tsin all styles seem to have been gathered up and exported under the general name of that port; just as in Japan, when from the port of Imari everything made at Arita and in the Hizen Province was shipped to Europe, the name of the port was given to wares that were never made there, but were only shipped from that place. It is therefore easy to understand the difficulties in the way of those handling the products of the past about which no records can be found. The face value of objects, and that only, can possibly avail.

THE prevalence of mythological animals in Chinese rug designs is a noteworthy feature. Dogs in vast numbers appear playing with balls and spherical objects which serve them as charms. Dragons seek their pearls, Ky-lins with sprays of fungus in their mouths lift their timid heads, and the gorgeous Fung-hwang lends its plumage to decorative effects. Mythical personages are represented by their emblems, these being floral or otherwise according to the legends about them interpreted in design. Things that symbolize ideas are meaningful as they

PLATE XIV.

Gold and azure rug.
[5585—6.10×4.0]

stand related to prevalent beliefs and superstitions, and a single flower or emblem may at once suggest some historic sequence or the relation of one important event to another.

THE use of certain designs at certain periods necessitates a constant reversion to the history of the Empire as the only means of obtaining a clue to the reasons why they were selected; for example, there are certain Mohammedan designs in products of the Kien-lung period which have borne without explanation the name of Kashgarian. This may be explained by the historic fact that one of the favorites of Kien-lung was a Kashgarian princess, for whom he ordered built a special mosque near the royal residence in Peking, and for whose use he procured much that was not in the least suggestive of the native religions in China or Buddhism, but savored wholly of Moslem thought and ideas.

PASSING to the consideration of the tendency to mingle mythological designs with geometric and naturalistic ornamentation, we find it impossible to secure any clue to the reasons for some of the combinations of styles. Very rarely is any definite plan demonstrated, as in an important rug in which a picture is reproduced in wools. In the details of the composition Perso-Chinese influences are introduced, but native Chinese superstition is illustrated in the design. It is considered an auspicious omen for swallows and sacred animals to approach a dwelling, as they are supposed to bring good luck and to avert evil.* In this design the deer is walking up the steps and birds hover over the roof of the house.

THE design in rug No. 8965 suggests the myths and legends of China connected with the sacred mountain rising from the waves, and has to do entirely with native design without outside influence of any kind whatever. The story of the sacred mountain lends itself to the imagination of the Chinese artist in whatever method of expression he adopts. In the olden days this

---

* The coming of swallows and their making their nests in a new place, whether dwelling house or store, is hailed as an omen of approaching success or a prosperous change in the affairs of the owner or occupier of the premises.—DOOLITTLE.

PLATE XV.

Swallow-myth rug.

[5432—6.0×4.5]

PLATE XVI.

Sacred deer rug.
[5568—9.5 × 5.7]

great mountain was considered the God of the Tartars. The Sacred Mountain of China, as it appears in ornament, is mythological, for while that land abounds in mountain peaks of interest, it is to the Mountain in design that allusion is here made. At the center of all things it arose from the ocean of eternity. It had to do with elemental conditions and was the first material manifestation when all was void. The mountain in Mongolian ornament is often pictured as having five peaks, sometimes only three. As an emblem in the hand of the Pearly Emperor and the Taoist priest, it is represented as a single peak, as is also the case when the symbol is held by Confucius. This emblem, together with the sceptre and the fungus, have become known and verified features in Chinese ornament.

MANY primitive peoples have believed that the souls of the righteous mounted to heaven from the branches of trees or high mountains, and for this reason revered mountains are sometimes pictured in early art as bearing a crest or crown of stars.

Star myths have in this way become in-
timately associated with legends of mountains,
and deities presiding over the events of life
are by imaginative mortals given special stars
for their abode. The clouds, too, form part
of the conventionalized ornament that bears
directly upon these considerations. In the
constellation of Ursa Major, the "Great
ruler" was supposed by the Mongolians to
reside.

IN sixteenth century carpets the cloud
forms representing this constellation
and the star circles themselves are
preserved, but in later copies the cloud form
remains with loss of meaning as a simple
ornamental design. The fungus, or Joo-e, is
sometimes mistaken for a cloud form in ornament, and care is necessary in deciphering
and determining forms and their derivation
and meaning. When the Mongolian Tartar,
three hundred years ago, wished to represent
Paradise, he threw over the field of his rug a
design which resembled twisted ribbons and
flowing bands, which threaded their way
through numberless cloud forms which connected small circles and discs representing

PLATE XVII.

Swastika medallion rug.

[5596—4.2 × 2.2]

stars. Later thought developed this design in East India and Persia, and Mohammedan influence introduced symbolic representations which deviated entirely from the original and early thought.

IN No. 4988, the dragon horse occupies the center of the field and lion dogs appear at either end. In No. 5448 the crane is pictured flying among the clouds, the messenger of the God of Longevity and the oft chosen symbol of mortal success. The wild swan, the wild goose, the stork and the crane figure in significant ways in rug designs as well as in other Chinese ornament. The white crane and the tortoise were supposed to dwell in the " Isles of the Genii," off the eastern coast of China, and they, with other emblems of longevity, are frequently portrayed in Chinese art.

RUG No. 5568* shows Persian influence in the treatment of the tree form, which rises from rocks and covers the entire field with spreading branches. On either side of the rocks are spotted deer, one of which holds a spray of sacred fungus in his mouth. A corrosive band surrounds the rug, and the colors, design and weave testify to its eighteenth century origin. Here we find the tree peony with the blossoms drawn in two ways, both of which are found in regular designs and are only different drawings of the same flower. The tree as such in Chinese rugs is extremely rare. As drawn in this rug, animals appear at its base. The significance is mythological and without doubt the intention is to denote the preference shown for special trees, fruits, etc., by the sacred animals. Here we find the deer with a spray of longevity fungus in his mouth as chosen food. Large butterflies feed on the leaves of the tree. In color this rug is most pleasing. The field of fawn color carries the tree and leaves in yellow tan. The blossoms, some of them, are light and some dark blue. Others are of varying shades of tan. The borders are harmonious and do not show the strong contrasts that sometimes prove disturbing.

CHAPTER VI.

THE CLASSIFICATION OF RUGS
ACCORDING TO DESIGN.

ILLUSTRATING geometric designs of the "early Ming" period, and those which combined archaic scroll, fret and animal designs formally arranged with the geometric, the following rugs furnish excellent examples: Nos. 3908, 4901, 4910, 4980, 5504, 5598, 5490, 4983. Rugs of this class invariably carry either plain bands of color, or simple geometric designs in the borders, and are apt to be surrounded by an outer limiting band of dark corrosive brown.

OF similar nature, great beauty of color, technical precision of weaving, but of different though typical design, is No. 5449. The warp and woof in this rug answer the requirements that this type of Ming product demands, and are crudely prepared. In both field and border a soft dull yellow tone prevails. Scattered over the field and occupying its entire surface, with the exception of the square central reserve measuring about 4 x 4 feet, is a repetitive design consisting of wavy dark brown lines. While not resembling tiger skin absolutely, this design bears that name. The central reserve, formed on the yellow ground by outlined bands of light and dark blue, is filled with crude and elemental designs, copied from the first or early period in the historic ornament of China. There are vases, copies of bronzes, receptacles for sacred fruits, objects and utensils of significance and several crudely drawn mythical monsters. The design in the border of the rug is of a most simple nature of geometric form. Sapphire and sky blue, tan, rich gold color, fruit red and corrosive brown are the colors found in this rug and others of the same period. These colors vary in tone, the earlier rugs having faded to softer shades or having been originally dyed in lower key. The robin's egg blue found in the oldest rugs of this style is of great beauty.

PLATE XVIII.

Cloud-band medallion rug.
[4971—9.4 × 6.9]

THOUGH much worn, rug No. 5573 shows in perfect condition the design of dark blue upon a tan background. The corners are geometric. Above and below the central medallion, which is entirely geometric, six archaic dragon-headed creatures with foliate and bifurcated tails, disport themselves. The outer border of corrosive brown has worn away so that the web is distinctly shown and may be compared with specimen rugs of the period. The colors as well as designs adhere to the type.

IN design, No. 5582 differs from others of the same class, as the central medallion and corner spaces are not geometric but are filled with archaic dragons or scrolls based upon them. Four geometric corners describe a square outside the central medallion. In No. 5574, six dragons surround a central medallion and a dragon form is in each of the four corners. This rug is surrounded by two geometric borders and one band of corrosive brown. No. 5565 shows in both medallion and inner corners geometric designs, and three dragons appear in the field at the top and bottom. These rugs, with a

few other well known authenticated specimens, constitute an honorable company of
antiques at whatever period they were woven.
They antedate any other Chinese rugs obtainable at the present time.

NO. 5567 gives an all-over octagonal
and square design with swastikas in
the intersections, and floral motifs in
each octagonal form. A running swastika
design is found in the single border. No.
5581* and No. 5505* are of the same period
of weaving but different in design. In both,
sacred objects are outlined on a plain field,
sacrificial cups, pots, jars and plates, fruits,
censers, receptacles for altar implements,
chess-boards, an abacus and stands for scrolls,
books, etc. The introduction of dull persimmon red in the inner border of this latter
rug is to be noted, as later the persimmon
shade deepened in rugs which were made as
copies of the older period. All the objects
used in design are of archaic form and the rug
is invaluable as a repository of the early and
significant art of China. Careful analysis of
the fabric gives conclusive and convincing
testimony concerning its age and merit.

E pass from the geometric styles of the late Ming and early K'ang-hsi periods into the later developments based upon Persian influence, which resulted in the conventionalization of floral and vegetable forms and in the gradual supplanting in the borders of archaic, by floral designs. First there was the substituting of only floral borders, then the placing of naturally drawn flowers around, above and below the central geometric medallion, where dragon scrolls (5475) or only conventionalized ornament had previously appeared. Several uses of this new style are noted in old rugs. In the corner spaces and medallions, geometric dragon forms are placed with flowers and butterflies between them (5508) and over the field copies of old bronzes are interspersed with fungus-looking growths, Buddha's fingers, peaches, stands, implements, etc., the wide border being floral.

IN No. 5526 are most carefully drawn objects, books, pencils, jars, censers and scroll stands. In No. 5528, both the scrolls and flowers in the corner, and central medallion illustrate the style, the only trace of the fret being in the corners. There

are two floral borders, one of which is composed of tripods, flowers, and stands, very
unusual and significant. The inner border is
dotted with signs of "shou." A cloud band
outlines the central medallion, and rocks are
shown in the design conventionally drawn.

NO. 5538 has larger and more highly
conventionalized flowers. In No.
5522 there is no floral border at all.
The corners and medallions show fret work,
but no suggestion of the dragon save the head.
In No. 5546 we lose entirely all geometric
forms, not even having the dot in the inner
border. Discs in the outer border are the
principal Chinese feature. No. 5499 belongs
to the strictly floral and precious objects
variety, only slight suggestion of scroll work
appearing in the central medallion. In the
design are peacock feathers, sprays of coral,
fans, etc. In No. 5516, six large floral forms
and four smaller ones fill the field. In the
inner medallion the Fung-hwang and the
dragon horse appear. In No. 5576* a floral
scroll is shown, combined with medallions and
corners of dragon scrolls. These extend all
around the border, alternating with a con-

PLATE XIX.

Moslem-blue rug.
[5467—8.3 × 5.3]

ventional form often copied from porcelains.

WE are led by a close study of floral designs to a careful consideration of the flowers themselves which are used in conventionalization. At first they look alike, but later, when subdivisions are in order, copies of Persian styles may readily be distinguished from those showing Chinese methods of conventionalization. The aster, peony, horse-chestnut, chrysanthemum, azalea and various orchids are sometimes drawn naturalistically but more often in a highly conventional manner.

PROCEEDING in the consideration of the application of design, we find that the use of a single medallion antedates the use of many medallions in the field. A late arrangement shows a well balanced ornament above and below the central medallion, so arranged as completely to fill the space. No. 5594 is thus arranged; No. 5596* also, though the latter has a central medallion in which are swastikas. There are swastikas in each corner and the design combines geometric and floral forms.

A MOST interesting combination of floral and dragon forms is shown in Rug No. 5487. Adapting designs to place is a feature of late eighteenth century work, examples of which may be noted in Nos. 5586, 5449, 5539, 5525, 5490, 5585*, 5517. While there are slight differences in arrangement, similar flowers are used in the same way in all of the rugs. In No. 5449 is a most powerful rendering of the heavy floral form called by some chrysanthemum and by other the mowtan or tree peony. In No. 5490 a more naturalistic drawing is noticeable, and cloud bands surround the medallion.

TREES and plants in boxes and jardinieres copy old designs in the field of rug No. 5453, but the border designs are late. In No. 5521, use is made of large blossoms in the design which is strictly floral. There are dashes of white in the foliations in the border of rug No. 5539 and a piquant fresh handling of the oft used peony motif. European influence is shown in the drawing of the design. In No. 5446 the central medallion appears with a wide encircling border, which serves as an outer rim. In the central space are mythological lions playing with their balls. In the corners, dragon-head scrolls are combined with a late rendering of the peony form.

FOLLOWING closely the development in the use of design, we find the appearance of several medallions laid either upon a plain or an all-over decorated field. These medallions became very elaborate in late eighteenth century rugs, and combined geometric, mythological and floral elements which are often meaningless and purely decorative, but perhaps more beautiful on that account, for the lack of symbolic design in Chinese art is not always considered a loss. The building up of these medallion forms is of interest, as the central ornament in them is often unrelated to their outer border.

IN No. 5566 a very simple use is made of five medallions, the center one being considerably larger than the others. Significant objects of one sort and another alternate with floral sprays which fill the field between the medallions. The outer border of the rug carries peonies with foliate ornamentation, and in the inner border is a T fret.

NO. 5542 is an eight medallion rug, and the floral design and butterflies are so arranged over the field as to give balance to the whole. Were it not for an occasional sign of "shou" in the broad border, there would be no suggestion of meaning in the design in this rug. The five medallion rug, No. 5515, has a symmetrically arranged field, an inner T border and an outer border showing peony foliation in the design. Light leaves and dark leaves, but no shaded leaves appear. In No. 5547 are four scalloped-edged medallions, and a large central floral medallion, formed of sprays of open blossoms and buds. Close analysis of these floral designs enables us to place the period of the rug itself. Comparison with porcelains shows exactly the same variations in treatment, use of shading, perspective, drawing, etc. and they all are as late as Kienlung and chronicle the story of European influence upon both potters and weavers.

PLATE XX.

Persimmon-color rug.
[5540—8.2 × 5.4]

IN this rug archaic dragons appear in the border, at the corners and at both sides. They face and guard one of the signs of "shou." Many of the Po-ku, or Hundred Antiques, and various other precious objects appear in the field of this rug; books in cases, a chess-board, a lute, partly covered, and scrolls, and the significant fruits, peach, pomegranate, etc. At the top and bottom of the field are jars in which sprays and branches are being forced for the New Year. Use is made in the five medallions of full-blown chrysanthemum or peony motifs without foliage; the corners are geometric. Both the borders show Samarcand and Mongolian influence. In No. 5537 a light-weight flower arrangement obtains in the medallions, but heavy, large blossoms are arranged across the field, interspersed by butterflies and the meaningful fruits, peach, pomegranate, etc.

PLATE XXI.

Grains-of-rice rug.
[5549—8.2 × 5.1]

PLATE XXII.

Nine lion rug.
[5468—8.3 × 5.6]

CHAPTER VII.

CLASSIFICATION OF RUGS
ACCORDING TO COLOR.

HAVING made most careful classification of rugs in strict adherence to methods suggested, so that it is possible to form an opinion at a glance as to which of the five great styles a design belongs, it is necessary, before determining the age of each rug examined, to study both color and weave in addition to the design. Only in this way is it possible to establish belief concerning the age of the specimen itself. For example, in rug No. 5454* both web and color sustain the opinion that the rug is an early eighteenth century specimen. The coloring is monotone in effect, although the imperial yellow field is checquered faintly with reddish brown, and light blue bands outline the central medallion and appear in the borders, giving great value to the accentuating tints. The corrosive brown is almost entirely gone and the designs are therefore thrown into high relief. Very little remains of the outer band that originally surrounded the entire rug. Examination of the materials used establishes the belief that the testimony of both color and design is correct, and that the fabric is of the early eighteenth century.

THE yellow color of the field in No. 5121 is the same as in No. 5454*, but because of the use of deep sapphire blue to the exclusion of all other colors in the design, the general tone of rug 5121 appears deeper than 5454*, and more like the rugs of an earlier period, bearing dragon scroll designs. Both of these rugs belong to the first great period in the classification of Chinese rugs, and are either late Ming or early K'ang-hsi weavings or copies of these styles made in the eighteenth century. Sometimes an older rug is better preserved than the later copy of it which has been much worn.

PLATE XXIII.

Literati rug.
[5479—9.1 × 5.9]

G IVING prominence to color instead of design, a study of Nos. 4978, 5588 and 5600 will lead the thought in a little different way. In No. 4978 we have in the field a brown red which has faded to a yellow. Dark and light blue and tan are the colors used in the design. In No. 5588 the ground is of a light tan, a shade which often is the result of time upon unbleached wool. Reds, blues and yellows are used in the design, which is most carefully worked out, showing many significant and interesting objects. Emblems following each other all around the border are drawn with Kien-lung accuracy and show great liberality in the use of color, for even a mandarin orange color is used in alternation with the lemon yellow generally found alone. Buddha's fingers, sprays of various sorts, baskets, urns, vases, ewers, and stands with fruit appear in the border designs. At first sight, the low tone this rug has acquired by natural fading makes one feel that it belongs to an earlier period than the close examination of colors proves to be the case. Both design and weaving belong to the eighteenth century, and presumably to its Kien-lung period.

IN archaic design has been used in No. 5119, which has been worked in light and dark apricot and yellow. The surface color is the result of fading, and of the disappearance of certain ingredients in the red dye, which has produced a dull yellow shimmer that is most wonderful in tone. There are occasional touches of two shades of blue and one of tan in the design. The piece is a Kien-lung specimen.

A COLOR study of several rugs, showing one or another rendering of the same idea of design, may be made by comparing the rugs Numbered 4539, 5122, 4791, 4886, 4377, 4381. Of several hundred Chinese rugs, these happen to be the only ones in which the sacred mountain appears in the design. Of these six rugs no two are of the same period of weaving, and they represent no less than three different periods, places and methods. No. 4377 is the latest of the lot, and is of coarse wool and crude colors. It is oblong in shape, of dark maroon color. Across the ends are diagonal lines in strong colors, copied from the brocade designs used on Mandarins' robes.

The pattern has been chosen and arranged without regard to significance, and Samarcand influences are plainly visible in the drawing of the waves and mountains. The diagonal lines representing water are in green, blue and reds. In No. 5123, the design is augmented by the presence of dragons which fill the field. The rug shows Chinese Turkestan coloring and influence, and belongs to a class sometimes called "Kashgarian."

WONDERFUL rendering of the sacred mountain and wave design appears in 4791. The whole color effect is yellow and blue, without trace of any of the pink or mandarin orange, which give an entirely different effect to the color scheme of No. 5123. In 4381, the design of the mountain itself is of corrosive brown. The ornamentation of the entire rug is composite, flowers being used in the corners to balance the design, in which fugitive colors were employed.

NUMBER 5122 shows a combination of geometric and floral patterns, so carefully balanced that they make a most pleasing design. In color the effect is imperial yellow, though the field itself is of a brownish yellow faded from apricot. The strong imperial yellow is used generously in the design, in which are also two shades of blue and cream color, with occasional touches of deep brown. This rug is easily, in design, color and weave, one hundred years old. The designs stand in high relief, produced by cutting away the wool around them, not in the more frankly confessed modern way, but according to native methods practiced in the Yung-cheng and early Kien-lung periods. Both weaving and color show the rug to be of a later period than the style would indicate.

IN blue and white Chinese rugs the shades range from the color of un-bleached wool verging on tan to the varying whites, *blanc de chine*, ivory, ash, putty and egg-shell. As rugs developed from the old tans and blues to the blue and white period, the shades vary with definite allegiance,— first to the use, in the designs, of deep, rich sapphire blues which were laid flatly on the white field in one color; and later to the combination with this dark blue of a light and very marvellous color known as robin's

PLATE XXIV.

Buddhist rug.
[5469—8.9 × 5.8]

egg blue. Rugs Nos. 5488*, 5125, 5469*, 5482, 5468*, 5479*, 5114, 5473, 5477, 5481, 5483, 5470 are all approximately of the same period. The two blues used in the design are almost identical in the various rugs, though in some the preponderence of the light blue gives rare charm and interest and closely simulates the early robin's egg blue.

THE distribution of the design in No. 5468* is most attractive, five lion dogs being symmetrically arranged in the field, the corners carrying the same animal design. So ingeniously are these mythological animals conventionalized that their backs and tails form sweeping light blue ornamentation, which spreads over the field as medallions are ordinarily distributed. Nos. 5114, 5479*, 5125, 5473, 5482, 5470, are single medallion rugs, while Nos. 5488* and 5477 carry eight medallions, and Nos. 5469* and 5483 have each five medallions.

THE central medallion in No. 5469* is different in nature from the four discs which surround it. A cloud band makes an outer circle, and the alternate light and dark blue clouds are very beautiful in color. Mythological animals in the two shades of blue are pictured in the various discs. The dragon horse, the Fung-hwang, lion dogs and stag with horns, mythological birds, pomegranates and other fruits are woven in rich dark blue, showing the seeds of the fruits, stems of leaves, etc., in contrasting light blue. Buddhist emblems appear in the border,— the wheel, the conch, the joo-e and the knot of destiny.

A STUDY of all these rugs together will show the similarities and differences between the blues used, and analysis of the colored wools makes it possible to determine accurately the period of manufacture. In No. 5114 the field is of clay or putty color. In quality, design and color, this small specimen reigns supreme, and with its companion No. 5115*, makes a notable pair. No. 5567 shows an introduction of persimmon red as ground for the inner floral stripe, and elsewhere in the design there is the addition of soft colors to the blue and white. In No. 5485, the combination of browns, yellows and reds in the border gives a decidedly polychrome effect, though the field is of tan white, over which a conventionalized peony design is spread in solid dark blue without shading. The persimmon red in the key pattern is true to period and style, and is quite unlike the crude shade that afterward appeared in copies of old rugs.

WHEN shading became popular, it is an interesting point to observe that it crept but slowly into geometric design. First it was introduced into the T border, and two shades of blue were used instead of one; but it was at a later period that the swastika fret yielded itself to the influence of the Italian school and assumed intricate and highly ornate forms. In No. 5593, the ground deepens to a full rich tan, and the shade of light blue in the border stripe is unusual. This rug has as its companion No. 5592, which duplicates it both in design and quality.

THE first feature of importance in rug No. 5567 that reveals itself to the observer is the skillful handling of the three colors—a pinkish red, dark blue, and yellow—in several of the discs, which rest upon the flower-strewn field without disturbing the harmonious effect. The disc at the lower left, in which a stag is drawn, is balanced by an animal subject in the disc at the upper right. The other corner discs carry floral designs, while in the larger central medallion two lions or dogs appear. While the color scheme of the rug is blue and white, the touches of red and yellow lend strength and individuality to the fabric, as do the over-glaze colors sometimes added to blue and white porcelains.

A STUDY of yellow, as used by the weavers of China from early times to the present, is of importance in the analysis of rugs, as many conclusive facts may be verified by close comparison of a great number of specimens. A few points of importance that lead to definite opinions are readily comprehended, and these conclusions may be applied to any groups of rugs, as interpretive and elucidating. The varieties of Chinese yellow are known as imperial, mandarin, tan, lemon, orange and citron, and it is significant that of these, lemon and citron

PLATE XXV.

Five medallion rug.
[5496—6.8 × 4.6]

yellow are rarely if ever found in rugs made prior to the eighteenth century, while antique yellows never have the greenish cast noticeable in late products.

ARLY Ming and K'ang-hsi yellows merge from dull tan color into conservative shades of strong yellow tan, which evolve into a rich gold color, and find illustration in No. 5133 and other rugs of the same class. Later the yellows became heavy with red, and the desired effect in the finished product was sometimes produced by hatching a ground of yellow with apricot color, or by dotting the surface with a "grains of rice" design in some soft shades of fruit red. No. 5128 illustrates this point. The color of the field thus secured is monotone in effect, though to produce it, use has been made of two distinct colors, yellow and apricot. The rug is marvellous in many ways, showing as it does the adherence to old designs taken from bronzes. These are shown in the discs, which, on a light robin's egg blue, carry archaic and symbolic designs similar to those found on the mirror backs of early dynasties.

NUMBER 5133 is an unusual and very fine rug. The robin's egg blue in the border and the dark blue in the floral sprays are superb, adding zest and vigor to the strong tone of the field which is of the K'ang-hsi tan yellow variety. There are many points of distinction in the technique of the weaving, which indicate the influence of the Yung-cheng period. In No. 5131 the designs are of great interest, several Buddhist emblems being among them — the gourd, the conch, the shell, the wheel, etc. Lion dogs are placed at intervals among the emblems, as though attracted by and guarding them.

IMPERIAL K'ang-hsi yellow — a strong, rich yellow of golden hue — is well shown in the lustrous wool of rug No. 5153*. Ten small discs rest upon a field of solid yellow, the further ornamentation consisting of flower forms symmetrically arranged as corners, and a floral border of great beauty. Varying shades of yellow are prevalent in the industrial arts of China, and in speaking of imperial yellow reference is made only to a color which bears that name. This does not necessarily suggest that the object was made for Imperial use.

THE field in No. 5521 deepens into full yellow of a shade that antedates that used in 5153*. Upon this field are designs that deserve close study. Jardinieres, vases of flowers and flower sprays appear. Emblems of the scholar surround the central disc,—a chess-board, books, a lute and scrolls. These designs are wrought in wonderful shades of blue. Yellow is preserved in the borders, thus making a most harmonious background for the designs in blue laid upon it. No. 5559 shows a tan yellow, and an apricot color that has faded to about the same shade. The ground of the border stripe is tan, ornamented with a double swastika fret in dark blue.

CHINESE DIRECTION AND COLOR SYMBOLISM

DIRECTIONS	SEASONS	COLORS	ELEMENTS	PLANETS	METALS
North	Winter	Black	Water	Mercury	Iron
East	Spring	Green	Wood	Jupiter	Lead, Tin
South	Summer	Red	Fire	Mars	Copper
West	Autumn	White	Metal	Venus	Silver
Middle		Yellow	Earth	Saturn	Gold

Extracted from Mayer's "Chinese Reader's Manual."

The divinity who resides in Ursa Major ; with Chinese drawing
of stars in constellation.

PLATE XXVI.

Archaic lion rug.

[5126—7.3 × 5.6]

DESCRIPTION OF PLATES.

PLATE I.

ARCHAIC bronze urn belonging to the early period of Chinese art, ornamented with archaic dragon and geometric forms of extreme interest. The lizard-like archaic dragon has been sufficiently conventionalized to show only the head, the long sinuous body having given place to a rectangular formation of irregular nature.

PLATE II.

UPON a field of ashen white, in rug No. 5115* the geometric design in two shades of blue terminates in dragon heads; while in No. 5462* the heads disappear entirely and the geometric design which has evolved from animal form alone remains. The field of this rug has faded to a surface of copper color, and the blues of two shades in the design are superb.

PLATE III.

THERE is an indication in the design of rug No. 5132* that motifs of ornament were rearranged especially for the use of weavers in the early Ming period. The rug itself is of the K'ang-hsi period in weave and color, though the design shows Ming use of archaic ornament. The formation of the fret in the border is unlike later drawing of the swastika. It consists of two T forms placed together in such a way as to form disconnected sections, quite unlike the running swastika fret of a later period. The six dragons are placed on the field most symmetrically, and their foliated bodies and bifurcated tails suggest the scroll work that was later based upon them. In color the rug belongs to the tan and blue variety. The corrosive brown in the limiting border has worn away the wool from the surface. The

PLATE XXVII.

Eight medallion rug.
[5488—10.6 × 5.6]

PLATE XXVIII.

Ten medallion rug.
[5153—14.10 × 7.8]

design claims greater age than the fabric, though the rug is an antique of rare quality and merit.

PLATE IV.

MYTHICAL monsters fill a large central form which is outlined in blue and corrosive brown. The main color of the rug is yellow, and a matchless blue and corrosive brown are introduced in the design. In the outer border the design stands out in high relief from the background, which has corroded. The central reserve, formed on the yellow field, observes the outline of an old mirror back. Nothing more significantly demonstrates the fact that designs in bronze were copied by weavers than the examination of the medallions which figure in the field of rugs. Although at first glance the discs scattered at regular intervals or in the center seem to bear close resemblance to each other, analysis of their formation will reveal the fact that they differ. They have been carefully selected, and invariably copy floral or geometric forms used by workers in bronze and porcelain. There are the lotus, the peony, the water-chestnut, and many star and octagonal formations that give names to the decorative forms evolving from them.

PLATE V.

ORIGINALLY brownish apricot, the surface of the field in rug No. 5581 has faded to a soft yellow. In the design are yellows of differing shades, dark and light blue, apricot and cream color. Though over thirty objects appear in the design, one of great interest, the Abacus, gives its name to the rug, because of the rarity of its use in design. Each object in the design is outlined with contrasting color which, while it accentuates, also softens the effect and blends details.

PLATE VI.

NUMBER 5509 is an old K'ang-hsi product of the eighteenth century, decorated with carefully drawn "precious objects" on a deep tan field. There are vases copied from old bronzes; receptacles for

PLATE XXIX.

Thirteen medallion rug.
[5536—8.5 × 5.2]

sacred fruits, plants and flowers; altar utensils and scrolls and other articles of great significance. The fading to dull yellow of wools originally an apricot color is a notable feature in rugs of this age and class. Fugitive colors of later date show none of the characteristics belonging to these old specimens.

PLATE VII.

A COMBINATION of geometric forms and dragons' heads is found in the central medallion, corners and border, in rug No. 5576. The field of the rug, which is of yellow tan, is seen through a conventionalized foliation which entirely covers it. Upon this cream-colored scroll work, large floral forms are laid in shades of blue. The design in the border belongs to the earliest period and consists in rectangular dragon forms between foliate scrolls. The brown dye has somewhat corroded the surface of the outer border. The fabric has been bound with velvet in order to protect the edge.

PLATE VIII.

UPON a deep rich yellow tan in rug No. 5580, divisions are bounded by dark blue forms in each of which is a significant object in a deeper shade of tan. Two bats in one space — a peach of longevity in another. The border in blue and tan carries a running swastika design.

PLATE IX.

ANOTHER of the blue and tan variety belonging to the early Ming school of design is rug No. 5579. An all-over swastika fret in blue is placed upon a field of tan. Bats in tan color are scattered over the fret, imposed upon it. A plain band of light blue surrounds the field, and in the wide border a running swastika fret appears in tan and blue.

PLATE X.

SHOWN in rug No. 4389 is a most wonderful rendering of primitive design, the fabric itself bearing evidence to several hundred years' existence.

Both warp and weft are of silk, and the pile also is of silk of fine quality. The field is of rich dark blue, and the designs are worked in soft shades of peach-blow, apricot, yellows and jade-green. Dragons with five toes, suggestive of those found on divining boards, are placed alternately with objects indicative of official life.

PLATE XI.

ANOTHER sumptuous rug of the Ming metal and silk variety is shown in No. 4736. The entire effect of color in this rug is silver and blue, made soft and delicate by age and the tarnish of the metal employed in the background. The design stands in relief upon this background and is worked in silk.

PLATE XII.

A CHINESE adaptation of foreign motifs gives great interest to the design in rug No. 5599. As interest and study in Chinese art increase it becomes more and more possible to note the parallelism that exists between the art of the Eastern and Western Orient. The outcome of the mingling of styles has produced very definite results, which may generally be traced to their respective sources. Occasionally, however, one is at a loss to account for certain individual rugs, the designs in which are difficult to trace. At first glance this appears to be an antique Kirman rug, so distinctive is its appearance, and so rigid and compact the fabric. Analysis of the weave strengthens this opinion. The design and color scheme are of the Chinese Turkestan variety, however, and indicate an East Indian origin. The web of the rug is cotton and the pile is of soft, fine wool. Whether a Kirman weaver adopted Chinese styles and colors, or a Chinese colorist adopted Kirman methods to Chinese designs cannot be fully demonstrated, but there is enough that is illustrative of both Chinese and Kirman styles to call this beautiful product of the loom a Chinese-Kirman rug. In the province of Fars in Southwestern Persia, rugs similar to this were made in the sixteenth century by the descendants of the Mongolians who centuries before had settled there.

PLATE XXX.

Sacred mountain mats.
a. [5122—2.2 × 2.3]
b. [5123—2.2 × 2.3]

PLATE XIII.

THE forcing of designs into compartments, wherein details could be symmetrically and conventionally arranged, was one of the features of the K'ang-hsi period; and in rugs made in the North of China during the reign of the great Emperor, a design known as the "western lotus" grew out of an effort to adopt western ideas and styles. In rug No. 3459 this design is shown to perfection. In some of the large temple rugs of the Kien-lung period it is used as a repeat, and lends itself most acceptably to whatever use is required.

PLATE XIV.

CONVENTIONALIZATION of a different sort is shown in rug No. 5585, where upon a yellow ground a most unusual flower design is laid in blue. The foliations are of the K'ang-hsi style, and are somewhat crude and angular. The rug both in weave and design differs from rugs of a later period which carry an all-over pattern of a more ornate character.

PLATE XV.

(Described in text, page 48)

PLATE XVI.

(Described in text, page 51)

PLATE XVII.

THE field of No. 5596 is of a soft golden yellow, and the ground of the main border has faded from apricot to a yellow not unlike that in the field. In border, corners, and central medallion the designs are geometric, but in the lower and upper parts of the field floral forms are symmetrically arranged.

PLATE XVIII.

NUMBER 4971 is of apricot color, and carries designs in yellow, cream color and persimmon red. Scattered over the field are sprays of orchids, sunflowers and other blossoms. The large flowers in the corners are drawn in early eighteenth century style.

PLATE XIX.

A FULLER expression of floral development in design is to be found in rug
No. 5467, in which a riot of bloom
is apparent and no formal or geometric
arrangement exists either in field or border.
This rug is of the dark blue variety and is a
superb specimen of the style. One of the
borders carries butterflies of many colors.
The treatment of the flowers in the design is
unusual. Many of them are drawn in pro-
file and delicately shaded. Great skill is
shown in composition and in the use of colors.

PLATE XX.

A WELL balanced design, in two shades
of blue and cream color, covers the
field in rug No. 5540 with delicate
tracery. The weaver of this rug has used
a full rich persimmon color, which rarely is
used as ground color, appearing more often
in border stripes. This one of the Chinese
fruit-reds is more unusual than any, and seems
to have different values according to the place
it occupies in a design.

PLATE XXI.

ILLUSTRATING the use of mythical animals in design is rug No. 5549, in which the Chinese lion or dog occupies the central medallion. The yellow field, with the exception of the corners, is covered with a grains-of-rice pattern which dots the surface with brown. In the outer border, a T pattern in two shades of blue rests on a dull, faded persimmon ground.

PLATE XXII.

NINE lions appear in rug No. 5468 upon a flower-strewn field. Most exceptionally beautiful blues in this rare old specimen are suggestive of a period when robin's egg blue, strongly tinged with green, was used with the rich dark blue of the Ming period. An inner dotted band immediately surrounds the field, separating it from the floral border in which the treatment of flowers and leaves shows great technical refinement and an attempt to introduce shading.

PLATE XXXI.

Foliate dragon medallion rug.
[5474—6.0 × 3.7]

PLATE XXIII.

A MANDARIN'S rug most skillfully wrought is rug No. 5479, carrying in the design emblems and objects of interest and significance. The chessboard, the lyre, scrolls and books suggestive of the literati, with plants and flowers forced for the New Year, are placed around a central medallion. The rug belongs to the blue and white variety. Surrounding the field are three borders, which show both floral and geometric designs.

PLATE XXIV.

MYTHICAL animals again appear in No. 5469, in medallions of great interest. The Ky-lin and Fung-hwang in two of the medallions and dogs or lions in the other two are drawn in shades of blue. The field of the rug is light tan color, and an ornate floral border carries Buddhist emblems tied with fillets. The knot of destiny, the wheel of the law, the conch shell, the urn, the twin fishes, the lotus, the canopy and the umbrella are all introduced.

PLATE XXV.

NUMBER 5496 is a five medallion rug with tan ground in both field and border. Upon this soft background floral discs are laid, and sprays of fruit-blossoms with butterflies are scattered over the intervening space.

PLATE XXVI.

ANTIQUE in style, color and design, No. 5126 challenges attention. Lions form the decoration of the corners; and in very lightly drawn medallions, no two of them alike, are floral sprays with an occasional jade ornament. The color — blue — is supreme, the rarest of all blues found in rugs — the real robin's egg blue of the seventeenth century. The field of the rug is yellow.

PLATE XXVII.

NUMBER 5488 is an eight medallion rug of the blue and white variety. The field has softened to a dull ashen hue, and the blues are strong and clear, though marvellously blended with each other. The designs are most skillfully shaded, showing all the refinements in process that were introduced by the early emperors of the present dynasty.

PLATE XXVIII.

A TEN medallion, imperial yellow rug is No. 5153, of a quality that lends beauty to every feature of the design which adorns it. Every effort has been made to crowd the field with ornament. Large chrysanthemums form the corner designs, and single blossoms are set on the field between the medallions. Two shades of blue, apricot, persimmon, yellow and cream color are used in borders and medallions. In color, design and quality the rug deserves to be classed "Imperial."

PLATE XXIX.

T HIRTEEN medallions are rarely found in a Chinese rug, and because of them rug No. 5536 is unique. The medallions in two shades of blue and cream are laid on a field of rich, ripened apricot tint. Floral sprays are distributed between the medallions over the field of the rug, and in the border large flowers, alternately cream color and apricot, are freely placed at intervals between foliations in two shades of blue upon a yellow background.

PLATE XXX.

NUMBERS 5122 and 5123 are a pair of Chinese mats in soft shades of yellow, blue and cream. The central floral design is bounded on four sides by a conventional arrangement of the sacred mountain rising from the waves.

PLATE XXXI.

UPON a tan field, carrying an all-over scroll design which has faded so as to be hardly distinguishable, a central medallion composed of archaic dragon forms is outlined in dark blue in rug No. 5474. Above and below the medallion, confining corners which carry the swastika, are dark blue foliate scrolls which show a tendency to per-

PLATE XXXII.

Gold and azure medallion rug.
[5522—6.10 × 3.9]

fectly balanced ornamentation. This rug is of particular interest, as it marks a late seventeenth century rendering of an earlier design. It is surrounded by a dark blue outer border instead of one of the corrosive brown customarily used in earlier specimens.

PLATE XXXII.

NUMBER 5522 corresponds in color and age with No. 5585 and were it not that a central medallion and corners, formed of a geometric arrangement of archaic dragons, have been introduced in the border, the designs in the rugs would be indentical. Even now they very closely resemble each other. The colorists of a later period introduced shading in the rendering of this design.

CHRONOLOGICAL TABLE.

Sung Dynasty	A.D. 960-1279
Yuan Dynasty	1280-1367
Ming Dynasty	1368-1643
Hung-wu	1368-1398
Chien-wen	1399-1402

MING DYNASTY—*Continued.*

Yung-lo	1403-1424
Hung-hsi	1425
Hsuan-tê	1426-1435
Chêng-tung	1436-1449
Ching-t'ai	1450-1456
T'ien-shun	1457-1464
Ch'eng-hua	1465-1487
Hung-chih	1488-1505
Chêng-tê	1506-1521
Chia-ching	1522-1566
Lung-ching	1567-1572
Wan-li	1573-1619
T'ai-ch'ang	1620
T'ien-ch'i	1621-1627
Ch'ung-chêng	1628-1643

CH'ING DYNASTY 1644-

Shun-chih	1644-1661
K'ang-hsi	1662-1722
Yung-chêng	1723-1735
Kien-lung	1736-1795
Chia-ch'ing	1796-1820
Tao-kuang	1821-1850
Hsien-feng	1851-1861
T'ung-chih	1862-1874
Kuang-hsü	1875-

INVENTORY '80